43 All Natural Meal Recipes to Help Cure Urinary Tract Infections:

The Medicine Free Solution to Your Problems

By

Joe Correa CSN

COPYRIGHT

© 2016 Live Stronger Faster Inc.

All rights reserved

Reproduction or translation of any part of this work beyond that permitted by section 107 or 108 of the 1976 United States Copyright Act without the permission of the copyright owner is unlawful.

This publication is designed to provide accurate and authoritative information in regard to the subject matter covered. It is sold with the understanding that neither the author nor the publisher is engaged in rendering medical advice. If medical advice or assistance is needed, consult with a doctor. This book is considered a guide and should not be used in any way detrimental to your health. Consult with a physician before starting this nutritional plan to make sure it's right for you.

ACKNOWLEDGEMENTS

This book is dedicated to my friends and family that have had mild or serious illnesses so that you may find a solution and make the necessary changes in your life.

43 All Natural Meal Recipes to Help Cure Urinary Tract Infections:

The Medicine Free Solution to Your Problems

By

Joe Correa CSN

CONTENTS

Copyright

Acknowledgements

About The Author

Introduction

43 All Natural Meal Recipes to Help Cure Urinary Tract Infections: The Medicine Free Solution to Your Problems

Additional Titles from This Author

ABOUT THE AUTHOR

After years of Research, I honestly believe in the positive effects that proper nutrition can have over the body and mind. My knowledge and experience has helped me live healthier throughout the years and which I have shared with family and friends. The more you know about eating and drinking healthier, the sooner you will want to change your life and eating habits.

Nutrition is a key part in the process of being healthy and living longer so get started today. The first step is the most important and the most significant.

INTRODUCTION

43 All Natural Meal Recipes to Help Cure Urinary Tract Infections: The Medicine Free Solution to Your Problems

By Joe Correa CSN

Starting a new diet is a great way to help prevent urinary tract infections and to heal some other health issues you might have overlooked. That's why I have created these delicious recipes that will help to prevent and treat urinary tract infections.

Preparing food doesn't have to be complicated at all. In fact, it can be quite easy, as easy as any snack. It's the best way to know exactly what you're eating and what ingredients are in what you eat.

The recipes featured in this book are healthy and great tasting. They are perfect for breakfast, lunch, or dinner. This book will help you create some breakfast classics like homemade Smoked Salmon Spread, Rice Pudding, and Avocado and Cashew Cream. You will also find some perfect smoothie ideas you can try as well.

The recipes included in this book also provide numerous options for a variety of salads from lentils to tuna and a variety of vegetable combinations so you can get rid of your urinary tract infections faster.

43 ALL NATURAL MEAL RECIPES TO HELP CURE URINARY TRACT INFECTIONS: THE MEDICINE FREE SOLUTION TO YOUR PROBLEMS

Breakfast Recipes

1.   Salmon Pâté

Ingredients:

2 salmon fillets (1 inch thick), boneless and skinless

½ tsp of dry rosemary

1/8 tsp of sea salt

¼ tsp of chili pepper, ground

1 tbsp. of fresh lemon juice

Olive oil

Preparation:

Wash and pat dry the salmon fillets. Cut into bite size pieces and set aside. Heat up the olive oil in a large skillet and add the salmon pieces. Cook for about ten minutes stirring constantly. Remove from the heat and transfer to a food processor.

Add the remaining ingredients into the food processor. Process well until nicely combined. Serve with some fresh vegetables or whole wheat crackers of your choice.

Nutritional information per serving: Calories: 240, Protein: 20g, Carbs: 1.2g, Fats: 16g

2. Detox Smoothie

Ingredients:

¼ cup of spinach, finely chopped

¼ cup of broccoli, finely chopped

1 tbsp. of walnuts, minced

1 tbsp. of hazelnuts, minced

2 cups of water

¼ tsp of ginger, ground

A handful of ice cubes

Preparation:

Combine the ingredients in a blender and blend for about 30 seconds. Serve cold.

Nutritional information per serving: Calories: 110, Protein: 17g, Carbs: 7g, Fats: 3g

3.   Avocado and Cashew Cream Purée

Ingredients:

2 whole eggs

2 egg whites

1 tbsp. of cashew butter

½ cup of skim milk

1 ripe avocado, roughly chopped

1 tbsp. of fresh mint leaves, finely chopped

A pinch of salt

Preparation:

Hard boil your eggs (about 10 minutes will be enough). Remove from the heat and allow it to cool.

Peel and cut the eggs. Mash with a fork. Separate the egg whites from yolks.

Peel and chop avocado. Place it in a blender. Add milk, eggs, egg whites, cashew butter, salt, and mint leaves.

Mix well for about 30 seconds. Serve cold.

Nutritional information per serving: Calories: 187, Protein: 12.8g, Carbs: 7g, Fats: 4.5g

4. Fresh Tomato Smoothie

Ingredients:

1 cup of fresh tomato juice

2 small tomatoes, peeled

1 tbsp. of walnuts

1 tbsp. of honey

1 tbsp. of sesame seeds

Preparation:

Place the ingredients in a blender and blend for 20 seconds. Serve cold.

Nutritional information per serving: Calories: 111, Protein: 7g, Carbs: 27g, Fats: 1g

5. Rice Pudding

Ingredients:

2 cups of skim milk (you can use almond milk for extra flavor)

½ cup of rice, precooked

1 tbsp. walnuts, finely chopped

1 tbsp. of hazelnuts, finely chopped

¼ tsp of salt

1 tsp of cinnamon, ground

½ tbsp. of sugar-free vanilla extract

Preparation:

In a medium sized saucepan bring 2 cups of milk to boil. Add the rice, nuts, salt, vanilla extract, and stir well. Cook for about 10 minutes, or until you get a creamy mixture. Stir in some cinnamon and remove from the heat. Allow it to cool in the refrigerator before serving.

Nutritional information per serving: Calories: 158, Protein: 14g, Carbs: 3g, Fats: 2g

6. Smoked Salmon Spread

Ingredients:

1 cup of smoked salmon slices

½ cup of ground almonds

½ cup of fresh parsley

1 tsp of dry oregano

2 garlic cloves, crushed

2 tbsp. of olive oil

¼ cup of water

1/8 tsp of salt

Preparation:

Simply combine the ingredients in a food processor and mix well for about 30 seconds. Serve promptly with celery, or crackers, or side of choice.

Nutritional information per serving: Calories: 245, Protein: 41.3g, Carbs: 2g, Fats: 18g

7. Lean Lentil Burgers

Ingredients:

¾ cup of lentils, soaked

1 small red onion, peeled and finely chopped

½ medium-sized sweet potato, grated

1 small red pepper, finely chopped

2 slices of whole grain, buckwheat bread

2 tbsp. of rice flour

2 tbsp. bread crumbs

1 tsp. chia seeds

1 tsp of parsley, finely chopped

½ tsp of cayenne pepper

Salt and pepper to taste

Olive Oil

<u>Other:</u>

4 whole grain burger buns

1 medium-sized tomato, sliced

1 small onion, sliced

Several lettuce leaves

Preparation:

Heat up two tablespoons of olive oil over a large frying pan on medium heat. Add finely chopped onion and stir-fry until translucent. Add chopped pepper and continue to cook for a couple of more minutes, or until softened.

Remove from the heat and set aside.

Meanwhile, briefly cook the lentils (10 minutes should be enough). Drain and cool for a while.

Combine all fried ingredients with the lentils in a bowl and mix. Using your hands, shape 4 patties for the burgers.

Heat up 4 tablespoons of oil over a medium-high heat. Fry the burgers for 3-4 minutes on each side.

Serve with tomato, sliced onion, and lettuce. Add ketchup, or mustard, or mayo to your preference.

Nutritional information per serving: Calories: 294, Protein: 16.4g, Carbs: 59g, Fats: 6g

8. Mixed Berries Smoothie

Ingredients:

1 handful of mixed wild berries of your choice

1 tsp. of Stevia sweetener

1 tsp of ginger, minced

1 glass of water

Preparation:

Combine the ingredients in a blender and mix well for about 20 seconds. Serve cold.

Nutrition information per 1 serving: Calories: 19 Protein: 0.5g, Carbs: 7g, Fats: 0g

9. Quick Coconut Cookies

Ingredients:

1 ½ cup coconut flour

1 cup rice flour

¾ cup of powdered stevia

3 eggs

6 tbsp. of honey (can be replaced with agave syrup)

2 tsp of baking powder

1 tsp of cinnamon

Preparation:

Preheat the oven to 300 degrees F. Place some baking paper over a baking sheet. Set aside.

Combine all dry ingredients in a large bowl. Gently whisk in the eggs, stevia, honey, and cinnamon. Mix well until smooth dough. Using your hands shape the cookies. Place on the baking sheet and bake for about 10-15 minutes.

Remove from the oven and allow it to cool for a while.

Nutrition information per 1 serving: Calories: 126 Protein: 1g, Carbs: 17g, Fats: 5.1g

10. Frozen Cherry Yogurt

Ingredients:

1 cup of cherry yogurt (can be replaced with vegan yogurt)

½ cup of fresh cherries

4 strawberries

2 tbsp. of honey

Preparation:

Combine the ingredients in a blender and mix well for 20 seconds. Pour in a glass and keep in the freezer for about 30 minutes. Serve cold.

Nutrition information per 1 serving: Calories: 110 Protein: 2g, Carbs: 21g, Fats: 1.5g

Lunch Recipes

11.   Cilantro Garlic Burgers

Ingredients:

2 cups of lentils, soaked

3 cloves of garlic, minced

½ cup of breadcrumbs (choose buckwheat bread)

¼ cup of Cheddar cheese (freshly grated is best, but whatever you have will work)

1 egg, beaten

2 cups of water

½ cup of rice flour

salt and pepper to taste

Preparation:

In a medium size bowl, mash lentils with folk then mix with garlic, breadcrumbs and cheddar cheese. Form into patties; set aside.

Whisk egg and water in a bowl and in another bowl mix the flour with a pinch of salt & pepper. Coat each patty gently with flour mixture, then dip into egg mixture bowl, then coat again with flour mixture. Heat olive oil over medium-high heat in a large skillet. Fry the burgers until lightly brown, about 2-3 minutes each side.

Serve on warm buckwheat bread or in a whole grain pita with cilantro, onion, tomatoes and whatever else you like – but this is optional.

Nutritional information per serving: Calories: 480, Protein: 38g, Carbs: 36g, Fats: 17g

12.   Wild Salmon Salad with Rice

Ingredients:

7 oz. brown rice

5 oz. wild salmon fillet

4 tbsp. of extra virgin olive oil

5 oz. cherry tomatoes, halved

1 medium-sized onion, finely chopped

1 tbsp. of fresh mint, finely chopped

1 tsp of turmeric, ground

¼ tsp of sea salt

Preparation:

Place the rice in a deep pot. Add three cups of water and bring it to a boiling point. Cook for 15 minutes over medium heat, stirring occasionally. Remove from the heat and cool for a while.

Using a kitchen brush, spread the olive oil over the salmon fillet. Sprinkle with some salt and wrap tightly in aluminum foil. Add some more water in a pot and place the salmon in it. Bring it to a boil and cook for five minutes. Remove the salmon and unwrap. Chill for a while and cut into bite-size pieces.

In a large bowl, combine the salmon with rice, cherry tomatoes, chopped onion, mint, and turmeric.

Season with some more sea salt and olive oil, toss to combine and serve.

Nutritional information per serving: Calories: 171, Protein: 20g, Carbs: 17.8g, Fats: 6g

13. Red Salmon Fillet

Ingredients:

1 pound of fresh salmon, sliced into 1 inch slices

½ cup of olive oil

1 tbsp. of garlic powder

½ tsp of sea salt

1 tbsp. of dry parsley

2 tbsp. of ground red pepper

1 small onion, chopped

1 lemon, sliced

Preparation:

Combine the olive oil, garlic powder, sea salt, dry parsley, and ground red pepper in a large bowl. Place the salmon slices in it, cover and marinate for about an hour.

Preheat the oven to 350 degrees F. Place the marinated salmon slices in a small baking dish. Bake in oven for 35 minutes. Remove from the oven, and serve with onions and lemon slices.

Nutritional information per serving: Calories: 240 Protein: 58g, Carbs: 0g, Fats: 17g

14. Grilled Chicken Breast with Ginger Sauce

Ingredients:

4 oz. chicken meat, skinless and boneless

2 tbsp. olive oil

Preheat a non-stick grill pan over medium-high temperature. Cut the chicken meat into a bite size cubes. Add to the skillet and stir-fry with the olive oil for about 10 minutes.

Remove from the pan serve with ginger sauce.

How to prepare ginger sauce

Ingredients:

½ ounce of ginger root, peeled and chopped

1 garlic clove, crushed

1 tbsp. of fresh lemon juice

1 tsp of apple cider vinegar

¼ cup of chopped onion

Preparation:

Combine the ginger sauce ingredients in a blender and mix well for 20 seconds. Keep in the refrigerator for at least 20 minutes before serving.

Nutritional information per serving: Calories: 157 Protein: 30.8g, Carbs: 0g, Fats: 3.5g

15. Chilean Sea Bass Fillets

Ingredients:

4 oz. fresh sea bass fillets

1 lemon, sliced

¼ cup of lemon juice

1 tsp of dry rosemary, ground

1 tbsp. of fresh parsley, finely chopped

¼ tsp of pepper

Preparation:

Wash and clean the fish. Pat dry and cut in half.

Combine the lemon juice, dry rosemary, fresh parsley, and pepper in a large bowl. Soak the fish fillets with the bowl mix and leave in the refrigerator for 30 minutes to one hour.

Meanwhile, preheat the oven to 320 degrees F. Spread some baking sheets over a baking dish and set aside.

Remove the fish from the refrigerator and transfer to the baking sheet. Add some of the marinade on top of the fillets and bake for 30 minutes.

Remove from the oven, sprinkle with some more marinade and serve with lemon slices.

Nutritional information per serving: Calories: 77 Protein: 11.5g, Carbs: 0.2g, Fats: 3.5g

16. Crab Stew

Ingredients:

1 cup of diced tomatoes

4 oz. of frozen crab meat

1 tbsp. of dried basil

1 cup of fat free fish stock

1 cup of water

Pinch of pepper

1 oz. of tomato paste

3 celery stalks, washed, chopped

1 finely chopped onion

4 garlic cloves, crushed

Preparation:

Heat up a non-stick frying pan, to a medium temperature. Add chopped celery, onions, and about 2 tbsp. of water. Stir-fry for about 10 minutes. Remove from the heat and transfer to a deep pot. Add the remaining ingredients and cook for about 1 hour over a medium temperature.

Serve warm.

Nutritional information per serving: Calories: 177 Protein: 15g, Carbs: 4g, Fats: 0.5g

17. Tomato Soup with Celery

Ingredients:

2 oz. tomato, peeled and roughly chopped

Pinch of pepper

1 celery stalk, washed and finely chopped

1 onion, diced

1 bay leaf

1 tbsp. of fresh basil, finely chopped

Fresh water

Preparation:

Preheat the non-stick frying pan over a medium-high temperature. Add the onions, celery, and fresh basil. Sprinkle some pepper and stir-fry for about 10 minutes, until caramelized.

Add the tomato and about ¼ cup of water. Reduce the heat to low and cook for about 15 minutes, until softened. Now add about 1 cup of water and bring it to a boil. Remove from the heat and serve with 1 bay leaf.

Nutritional information per serving: Calories: 21 Protein: 0.7g, Carbs: 4.9g, Fats: 0.9g

18. Grilled button mushrooms

Ingredients:

4 oz. button mushrooms

1 tsp fresh dill

½ tsp of garlic powder

Preparation:

Preheat a non-stick grill pan over a medium-high temperature. Clean, wash, and cut each mushroom in half. Grill for 5 minutes while stirring constantly. Remove the mushrooms from the heat and transfer to a serving platter. Sprinkle with some garlic powder and top with fresh dill. Serve warm.

Nutritional information per serving: Calories: 119 Protein: 22g, Carbs: 1.5g, Fats: 1.7g

19. Mesclun Salad with Mussels

Ingredients:

4 oz. fresh mussels, de-bearded

1 onion, peeled and finely chopped

1 garlic clove, crushed

5 tbsp. of fresh lemon juice

¼ cup of fresh parsley, finely chopped

1 tbsp. of rosemary, finely chopped

1 oz. lettuce

1 oz. of arugula leaves

1 medium cherry tomato, for decoration

Sea salt to taste

Preparation:

Rinse and drain the mussels. Set aside.

Heat up a non-stick frying pan over medium-high temperature. Peel and finely chop the onion. Reduce the heat to medium temperature and add the chopped onion.

Add about ¼ cup of water. Stir-fry for several minutes, until crisp-tender. Now add the mussels and finely chopped parsley. Cook for about 20 minutes, stirring regularly. When all the water has evaporated, add garlic and chopped rosemary and stir well again.

In a large salad bowl, combine the mussels with arugula and lettuce. Add the lemon juice, sprinkle with some salt, and decorate with one cherry tomato. Serve promptly.

Nutritional information per serving: Calories: 78 Protein: 17g, Carbs: 6g, Fats: 9g

20. Thai Mushrooms with Ginger

Ingredients:

1 cup of Gouda cheese, chopped into cubes

3 tbsp. of ginger sauce

1 tbsp. of extra virgin olive oil

2 tbsp. of fresh ginger, ground

2 cloves of garlic

2 tbsp. of minced fresh chili peppers

½ cup of fresh button mushrooms

1 cup of fresh yellow pepper, chopped

1 cup of green beans, cooked

2 tbsp. of teriyaki sauce

¼ cup of water

¼ cup of fresh basil, chopped

1 small onion, peeled and sliced

2 cups of brown rice, precooked

Preparation:

Combine the ingredients in a non-stick frying pan or a wok. Heat up the stove to a medium temperature and fry the ingredients for about 20 minutes, while stirring constantly.

Serve with brown rice.

Nutritional information per serving: Calories: 157 Protein: 30g, Carbs: 29g, Fats: 11.9g

Dinner Recipes

21. Warm Quinoa and White Beans

Ingredients:

1 cup of quinoa, precooked

1 cup of white beans, precooked

3 tbsp. of hazelnuts, roasted

½ cup of fresh parsley

1 small onion, peeled and chopped

2 garlic cloves

¼ tsp of salt

5 tbsp. of extra virgin olive oil

1 cup of button mushrooms, sliced

¼ cup of cranberries, dry

Preparation:

Combine the hazelnuts, parsley, salt and 3 tbsp. of olive oil in a food processor. Blend well for 30 seconds. Heat up the remaining olive oil in a large skillet. Add chopped onion and garlic. Stir well and fry for several minutes, until nice golden color. Add cooked quinoa, white beans, button mushrooms, and mix well. Cook and stir for 5 more minutes, until the water evaporates. Remove from the heat and transfer to a large bowl. Add hazelnut blended mixture and ¼ cup of cranberries. Mix well and serve warm.

Nutritional information per serving: Calories: 189 Protein: 26.9g, Carbs: 39.6g, Fats: 8.9g

22. Mediterranean Sea Bream

Ingredients:

2 pounds of fresh sea bream

½ cup of extra virgin olive oil

1 whole lemon, sliced

4 rosemary sprigs

1 tbsp. of dry mint, ground

3 garlic cloves, crushed

¼ tsp of red pepper

Salt to taste

Preparation:

Wash and clean the fish. Cut lengthwise and remove entrails. In a medium bowl, combine the olive oil with dry mint, crushed garlic cloves, and red pepper. Brush the fish with this mixture and stuff with lemon slices and rosemary sprigs.

Place 2 tablespoons of olive oil on a non-stick frying pan. Heat up the stove to a medium temperature and fry the fish for about 6 minutes on each side.

Nutritional information per serving: Calories: 117 Protein: 17g, Carbs: 0g, Fats: 7.5g

23. Chicken Breast with Garlic and Parsley

Ingredients:

1 large chicken breast piece, skinless and boneless, cut into 1-inch-thick pieces

¼ cup of extra virgin olive oil

3 garlic cloves, crushed

½ cup of fresh parsley leaves

1 tbsp. of fresh lime juice

Salt to taste

Preparation:

In a medium bowl, combine the olive oil with crushed garlic cloves, finely chopped parsley, fresh lime juice and some salt (about ¼ tsp will be enough). Wash and pat dry the chicken meat and cut into 1-inch-thick pieces. Pour the olive oil mixture over the meat and let it stand for about 15 minutes.

Preheat the grill pan over a medium temperature. Add some marinade in the grill pan (about 2 tbsp.), then add the chicken fillets and cook for about 15 minutes while stirring occasionally.

Remove from the pan and serve with some vegetables of your choice.

Nutritional information per serving: Calories: 146 Protein: 33g, Carbs: 0g, Fats: 6.9g

24. Oven Baked Veal with Sweet Cabbage

Ingredients:

8 oz. veal cutlets

17 oz. sweet cabbage, shredded

1 small onion, finely chopped

1 garlic clove, crushed

¾ cup of fresh tomato paste

1 medium-sized red pepper, sliced

½ tsp. salt

¼ tsp of ground black pepper

Olive oil

Preparation:

Preheat the oven to 350 degrees F. Spread some olive oil over a baking dish and place the cutlets in it. Bake for 20 minutes, or until lightly charred.

Meanwhile, heat up two tablespoons of olive oil in a large skillet on medium-high. Add the onion and crushed garlic. Stir-fry for 2-3 minutes, stirring constantly. Now add cabbage, sliced pepper, and fresh tomato paste. Cover and reduce the heat to medium-low. Cook for about 15 minutes. Remove from the heat and set aside.

Remove the cutlets from the oven and add cabbage mixture onto the cutlet baking dish. Season with some salt and ground black pepper. Cover the baking dish with aluminum foil and return to the oven. Bake for 30 minutes then serve.

Nutritional information per serving: Calories: 118, Protein: 8.7g, Carbs: 9.1g, Fats: 5.4g

25. Sweet Potato and Peas Patties

Ingredients:

1 cup of green peas, cooked

1 sweet potato

½ cup of Parmesan cheese

½ cup of breadcrumbs

½ tsp. of salt

¼ tsp of freshly ground black pepper

1 egg

4 tbsp. of olive oil

Preparation:

Slice the sweet potato into one-inch-thick slices. Place in a deep pot and add enough water to cover. Bring it to a boil and cook until tender, for about 10-15 minutes. Remove from the heat, drain and allow to cool.

Transfer the cooked sweet potato slices to a food processor. Add green peas and process until smooth purée. Remove from the food processor and add salt, one egg, and black pepper. Mix well with a fork and using your hands, shape patties.

Heat up some olive oil in a medium-sized skillet. Roll each patty in breadcrumbs and fry for about three minutes on each side. Top with Parmesan cheese and serve.

Nutritional information per serving: Calories: 365, Protein: 12.4g, Carbs: 54.6, Fats: 14.1g

26. Celery with Gorgonzola

Ingredients:

½ cup of celery, finely chopped

1 medium-sized pear, sliced

½ cup of toasted almonds

½ cup gorgonzola cheese, chopped

For the dressing:

1 medium-sized orange, juiced

3 tsp. of horseradish

2 tsp. of honey

1 garlic clove, crushed

½ tsp. salt

¼ tsp. ground pepper

2 tbsp. of olive oil

Preparation:

Combine the dressing ingredients in a glass jar with a tight lid. Lock the lid and shake well to combine. Set aside.

Place the sliced pear on a serving bowl. Add chopped celery, toasted almonds, and chopped gorgonzola. Toss to combine.

Drizzle with dressing and serve cold.

Nutritional information per serving: Calories: 302, Protein: 4.5g, Carbs: 21.3g, Fats: 19.8g

27. Simple Lobster Recipe

Ingredients:

1 whole lobster

¼ cup of extra virgin olive oil

1 tbsp. of ground red pepper

½ tsp. of sea salt

¼ tsp. of black pepper

Preparation:

Preheat the oven to 350 degrees F. Meanwhile, combine the olive oil with sea salt, ground red pepper, and ground black pepper. Wash and cut the lobster in half along the long side. Place the lobster on a baking sheet and pour this mixture over it. Cook for about 10 minutes, until lightly golden color. Serve warm.

Nutritional information per serving: Calories: 111 Protein: 20g, Carbs: 0g, Fats: 6g

28. Roasted Veggies with Grated Cheddar

Ingredients:

½ cup of beetroot, peeled and diced

½ cup of green beans, cooked and drained

½ cup of Brussel sprouts, chopped

½ cup of pumpkin, peeled and chopped

½ cup of carrot, chopped

1 cup of fresh tomatoes, roughly chopped

1 small onion, sliced

½ cup of cooked lentils

2 garlic cloves, minced

1 cup of finely chopped silver beet

Pinch of salt and pepper

3 tbsp. of olive oil

1 cup of grated Cheddar cheese

Preparation:

Preheat the oven to 350 degrees F. In a large bowl, combine beetroot, green beans, Brussel sprouts and pumpkin. Add 1 tbsp. of olive oil and some salt to taste. Place on an oven tray and bake for about 20 minutes.

Meanwhile, heat up the remaining oil in a medium sized saucepan. Add onions and carrot and fry for about 5 minutes, stirring constantly. Add diced tomatoes and chopped silver beet. Season with pepper and gently simmer for about 20 minutes.

In a large serving bowl, place the precooked lentil and top with the fried mixture. Serve the lentils topped with the roasted vegetables, and cheddar cheese.

Nutritional information per serving: Calories: 195 Protein: 32g, Carbs: 35g, Fats: 10.9g

29. Spinach Muffins

Ingredients:

1 ½ cup of buckwheat flour

½ cup of rice flour

1 tbsp. of baking powder

½ tsp of salt

1 cup of skim milk

2 eggs

¼ cup of olive oil

¼ cup of sour cream

¼ cup of spinach, cooked

Muffin molds

Preparation:

In a large bowl, combine all dry ingredients. Gently whisk in milk and crack 2 eggs. Mix very well, even with an electric mixer. This will give you a nice, smooth muffin dough. Now add spinach and sour cream into the dough and mix well again. Shape the muffins using muffin molds.

Preheat the oven to 300 degrees F. Bake muffins for about 20 minutes.

Nutritional information per serving: Calories: 174 Protein: 9g, Carbs: 21g, Fats: 7.8g

30. Thai Trout

Ingredients:

1 pound of fresh trout

1 cup of fish stock

½ cup of olive oil

1 tbsp. of ground turmeric

½ cup of chopped celery

2 garlic cloves, crushed

2 tbsp. of fresh lime juice

¼ tsp of sea salt

1 cup of Thai vegetable mix, for serving

Preparation:

Wash and clean the trout. Pat dry and set aside.

In a deep pot, combine the fish stock with all the other ingredients. Bring it to boil and add the trout. Boil for about 10 minutes.

Meanwhile, heat up the grill pan over a medium temperature. Remove the fish from the pot and transfer to a grill pan. Add ¼ cup of fish stock in the pan and fry for several minutes.

Serve with Thai vegetable mix.

Nutritional information per serving: Calories: 287 Protein: 34g, Carbs: 9g, Fats: 12g

Salad Recipes

31. Veal Salad with Fresh Veggies

Ingredients:

1 pound of veal cutlets

1 large tomato, chopped

1 large green pepper, chopped

½ cup of cabbage, grated

2 tbsp. of olive oil

Pinch of salt

Preparation:

Heat up the olive oil over medium temperature in a large frying pan. Fry the veal cutlets for about 10 minutes on each side. Remove the veal and cut further into bite size pieces and combine with the grated cabbage, green pepper, and chopped tomato in a large salad bowl. Add some salt to taste and serve.

Nutritional information per serving: Calories: 247 Protein: 44g, Carbs: 14g, Fats: 17g

32. Homemade Tuna Salad

Ingredients:

1 (12oz) tuna steak

¼ cup of spring onions, chopped

4 tbsp. of extra virgin olive oil

¼ tsp. of sea salt

¼ tsp. of chili pepper

1/8 tsp. of white pepper, ground

1 tbsp. of fresh lemon juice

Preparation:

Heat up two tablespoons of extra virgin olive oil over a medium-high temperature on a large skillet. Season the tuna steak with chili pepper, white pepper, and salt, and then place on skillet. Cook for 5 minutes on each side.

Remove from the skillet and cool for a while. Flake the tuna steak into small pieces and mix with spring onions in a large bowl. Top with two tablespoons of olive oil and sprinkle with fresh lemon juice. Serve warm or cold.

Nutritional information per serving: Calories: 212 Protein: 25g, Carbs: 14g, Fats: 11g

33. Lettuce and Tomato Salad

Ingredients:

2 oz. tomato, roughly chopped

1 oz. lettuce, finely chopped

1 tsp. of apple cider vinegar

¼ tsp. of sea salt

½ tbsp. extra virgin olive oil

Preparation:

Place the chopped tomatoes and lettuce in a large salad bowl and toss. Season with salt, apple cider vinegar and olive oil, and then serve.

Nutritional information per serving: Calories: 19 Protein: 1g, Carbs: 7g, Fats: 7g

34. Chicken Salad

Ingredients:

3 skinless, boneless chicken breast halves

1 cup of chopped lettuce

1 medium onion, peeled and sliced

5 cherry tomatoes

2 tbsp. of low fat sour cream

1 tbsp. of olive oil

1 tsp. of chopped parsley

1 tbsp. of extra virgin olive oil

1 tsp. of minced chili pepper

1 tbsp. of lemon juice

Pinch of salt to taste

Preparation:

Cut the chicken breast halves into small cubes. In a medium bowl, mix the olive oil, chopped parsley, minced chili pepper and lemon juice to make a marinade sauce.

Put the chicken cubes on a baking sheet, sprinkle with marinade and bake at 350 degrees F for about 25 minutes. Remove from the oven. And let cool.

Meanwhile, in a large salad bowl, mix cherry tomatoes with chopped lettuce, sliced onion and low fat cream. Toss with chicken cubes, season with salt and olive oil and serve.

Nutritional information per serving: Calories: 187 Protein: 21.4g, Carbs: 7g, Fats: 2.5g

35. Arugula Salad with Berries

Ingredients:

2 oz. fresh arugula

1 orange, peeled and sectioned

5 fresh strawberries, squared

¼ cup of fresh blueberries

1 tbsp. of honey

3 tbsp. of fresh lime juice

5 tbsp. of fresh orange juice

¼ tsp of ground cinnamon

Preparation:

In a small bowl, whisk together 1 tablespoon of honey with fresh lime juice, fresh orange juice, and ground cinnamon. In a large salad bowl, place the berries and strawberry squares and the arugula, then mix. Top the salad with the honey mixture and toss. Serve cold.

Nutritional information per serving: Calories: 72 Protein: 3g, Carbs: 19g, Fats: 3.7g

36. Spring Onions Salad

Ingredients:

3 spring onions, finely chopped

¼ cup of sweet corn

1 tbsp. of fresh lime juice

2 tbsp. of olive oil

¼ tsp of salt

Preparation:

To prepare the onions you need to trim the roots away and strip off any extra outer leaves, then wash well. In a salad bowl, add two tablespoons of oil and place the chopped onions. Wait about 1 minute for the onions to absorb the oil and soften. Top with the sweet corn and mix together. Sprinkle with fresh lime juice and serve.

Nutritional information per serving: Calories: 122 Protein: 3.5g, Carbs: 21g, Fats: 7g

37. Colorful Bean Salad

Ingredients:

1 cup of cooked beans of your choice

½ cup of sweet corn

3 spring onions, chopped

1 small red pepper, finely chopped

1 small green pepper, finely chopped

¼ tsp. of cilantro

½ tsp. of red wine vinegar

1 tsp. of fresh lemon juice

3 tbsp. of extra-virgin olive oil

A pinch of salt

Preparation:

In a small bowl, mix the olive oil with red wine vinegar, fresh lemon juice, cilantro, and a pinch of salt. In a large salad bowl, toss together the corn, cooked beans, and the peppers. Top with the olive oil mixture and serve.

Nutritional information per serving: Calories: 220 Protein: 24g, Carbs: 32g, Fats: 11g

38. Baby Spinach Salad

Ingredients:

1 cup of cherry tomatoes

½ cup of Swiss cheese, cubed

1 cup of baby spinach

1 small orange, cubed

1 tbsp. of Parmesan cheese

1 tsp. of fresh lemon juice

Preparation:

Combine the ingredients in a large bowl and top with lemon juice. Mix well and serve.

Nutritional information per serving: Calories: 131 Protein: 20.5g, Carbs: 18g, Fats: 14g

39. Purple Salad

Ingredients:

1 piece of turkey breast, boneless and skinless

2 eggs

1 cup of red cabbage, grated

1 medium tomato, chopped

½ cup of olives

1 cup of scallions, chopped

½ cup sweet corn

4 tbsp. of olive oil

Pinch of salt

1 tbsp. of fresh lemon juice

Preparation:

Wash and pat dry the turkey meat then cut into 1-inch-thick strips. In a large skillet, heat up 2 tablespoons of olive oil on medium-high. Fry the turkey strips for about

10 minutes, turning them on all sides. Remove from the heat and transfer to a large salad bowl.

Meanwhile boil the eggs for about 7-8 minutes. Remove from the heat, drain and peel. Cut into slices.

Add the sliced eggs, chopped scallions, olives, chopped tomato, grated cabbage and sweet corn into the salad bowl with the fried turkey and mix well. Season with some salt and fresh lemon juice.

Nutritional information per serving: Calories: 186 Protein: 42g, Carbs: 38g, Fats: 17g

40. Sweet Corn and Tuna Salad

Ingredients:

2 cups of tuna, oil removed

½ cup of sweet corn

½ cup of red beans, precooked

1 small onion, chopped

¼ tsp of ground black pepper

¼ tsp of sea salt

1 tbsp. of olive oil

1 tbsp. of lemon juice

Preparation:

Peel and chop the onion into small pieces. Place the chopped onion in a salad bowl with the tuna and sweet corn. Add the precooked red beans and ground pepper and mix well. Season with olive oil, salt and lemon juice. Keep in the refrigerator for about 20-30 minutes before serving to serve cool.

Nutritional information per serving: Calories: 287 Protein: 31.7g, Carbs: 12.8g, Fats: 16g

Dessert Recipes

41. Chocolate Cake with Strawberries

Ingredients:

2 cups of all-purpose flour

3 tsp. of baking powder

3 cups of milk

2 large bananas, mashed

2 cups of raw cocoa powder

5 tbsp. of agave syrup

3 tsp of vanilla extract

2 oz. fresh strawberries, chopped

Preparation:

Preheat oven to 350 degrees F. Use a small baking dish (8x8 inch) and place some baking paper in it.

Mix together all ingredients in a large bowl, except the strawberries. Add agave syrup, mashed bananas, and vanilla extract and slowly whisk in the milk. Mix well with an electric mixer. Now add the chopped strawberries and using a spoon mix again.

Pour the mixture evenly into your baking dish and bake for about 45 minutes. Remove from the oven and allow it to cool for a while before serving.

Nutritional information per serving: Calories: 487 Protein: 35g, Carbs: 45g, Fats: 24g

42. Chocolate Brownies

Ingredients:

2 cups all-purpose flour

¼ cup of olive oil

½ cup brown sugar

1 cup of cocoa powder

1 large banana, mashed

2 tsp. baking powder

Preparation:

Mix all the ingredients in a large bowl using an electric mixer. Preheat the oven to 350 degrees F. Place some baking paper over a baking sheet. Bake for about 15 minutes, then cut into brownie square pieces and serve.

Nutritional information per serving: Calories: 243 Protein: 2.7g, Carbs: 39g, Fats: 10.1g

43. Dairy-free Chocolate Strawberry Dessert

Ingredients:

2 (12oz) cans of coconut milk

2 tbsp. stevia sweetener

2 tsp. of liquid strawberry extract

¼ tbsp. of salt

2 tbsp. of cornstarch

1 tbsp. chocolate sprinkles

12 chocolate cookies, crushed

Preparation:

Combine the coconut milk, sugar, salt, and cornstarch in a medium-sized pot. Bring it to a boiling point, over a medium heat. Cook for five minutes stirring constantly. Remove from the heat and cool well in the refrigerator for 10 minutes. Add the strawberry extract and beat well with electric mixer. Top with some crushed chocolate cookies and chocolate sprinkles and mix. Serve and enjoy.

Nutritional information per serving: Calories: 148 Protein: 1g, Carbs: 17.8g, Fats: 4g

ADDITIONAL TITLES FROM THIS AUTHOR

70 Effective Meal Recipes to Prevent and Solve Being Overweight: Burn Fat Fast by Using Proper Dieting and Smart Nutrition

By

Joe Correa CSN

48 Acne Solving Meal Recipes: The Fast and Natural Path to Fixing Your Acne Problems in Less Than 10 Days!

By

Joe Correa CSN

41 Alzheimer's Preventing Meal Recipes: Reduce or Eliminate Your Alzheimer's Condition in 30 Days or Less!

By

Joe Correa CSN

70 Effective Breast Cancer Meal Recipes: Prevent and Fight Breast Cancer with Smart Nutrition and Powerful Foods

By

Joe Correa CSN

www.ingramcontent.com/pod-product-compliance
Lightning Source LLC
Chambersburg PA
CBHW052121070526
44586CB00016B/2035